ALL ABOUT RATTLESNAKES

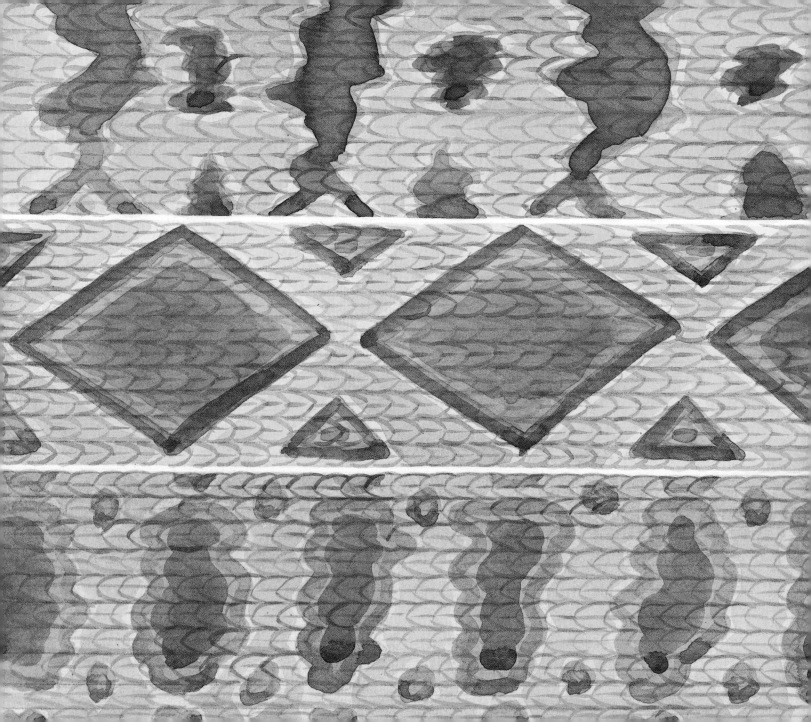

ALL ABOUT

Jim Arnosky

SCHOLASTIC INC.
New York Toronto London Auckland Sydney
Mexico City New Delhi Hong Kong Buenos Aires

Snakeskin patterns on the previous page:
Timber Rattlesnake (top)
Eastern Diamondback Rattlesnake (middle)
and Western Massasauga Rattlesnake (bottom)

RATTLESNAKES

Turn the next two pages to see a life-size portrait
of an Eastern Diamondback Rattlesnake.

ISBN 0-439-37617-3

12 11 10 9 8 7 6 5 4 3 2 1   2 3 4 5 6 7/0

Printed in the U.S.A.   08

First Scholastic trade paperback printing, March 2002

The artwork for this book was painted in watercolor.

For Luci and Bob

Have you ever wondered about rattlesnakes?
How dangerous are they?
Do rattlesnakes bite people?
Where do rattlesnakes live?
How many kinds of rattlesnakes are there?

This book answers all these questions and more.
It is all about rattlesnakes!

Timber Rattlesnake

Rattlesnakes are poisonous reptiles. They use their poisonous bites to kill the small animals they hunt and eat. They also strike out and bite to defend themselves. Because they are poisonous and will bite, rattlesnakes are frightening to people. They are also fascinating.

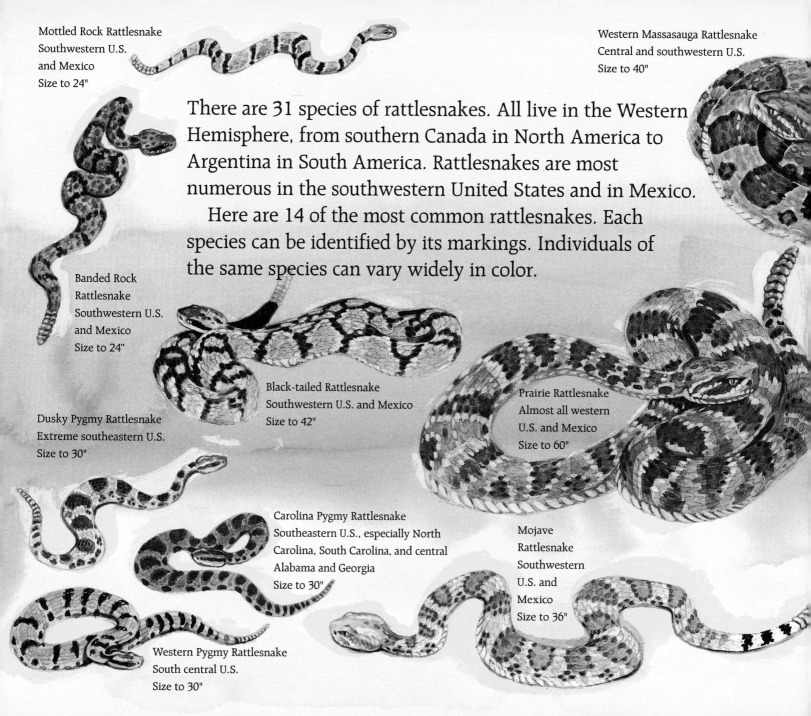

Mottled Rock Rattlesnake
Southwestern U.S.
and Mexico
Size to 24"

Western Massasauga Rattlesnake
Central and southwestern U.S.
Size to 40"

There are 31 species of rattlesnakes. All live in the Western Hemisphere, from southern Canada in North America to Argentina in South America. Rattlesnakes are most numerous in the southwestern United States and in Mexico. Here are 14 of the most common rattlesnakes. Each species can be identified by its markings. Individuals of the same species can vary widely in color.

Banded Rock
Rattlesnake
Southwestern U.S.
and Mexico
Size to 24"

Black-tailed Rattlesnake
Southwestern U.S. and Mexico
Size to 42"

Prairie Rattlesnake
Almost all western
U.S. and Mexico
Size to 60"

Dusky Pygmy Rattlesnake
Extreme southeastern U.S.
Size to 30"

Carolina Pygmy Rattlesnake
Southeastern U.S., especially North
Carolina, South Carolina, and central
Alabama and Georgia
Size to 30"

Mojave
Rattlesnake
Southwestern
U.S. and
Mexico
Size to 36"

Western Pygmy Rattlesnake
South central U.S.
Size to 30"

Timber Rattlesnake
(Black phase)
Midwestern, central, and northeastern U.S.
Size to 75"

Timber
Rattlesnake
(Yellow phase)
Midwestern, central,
and northeastern U.S.
Size to 75"

Eastern Massasauga Rattlesnake
Midwestern U.S. into Pennsylvania and New York
Size to 40"

Canebrake
Rattlesnake
South central to
southeastern U.S.
Size to 60"

Western
Diamondback
Rattlesnake
Southwestern
U.S. and Mexico
Size to 84"

Because of their large size
and abundance of venom,
Diamondbacks are
considered the most
dangerous snakes in the
world.

Eastern Diamondback
Rattlesnake
Extreme south-
eastern U.S.
Size to 84"

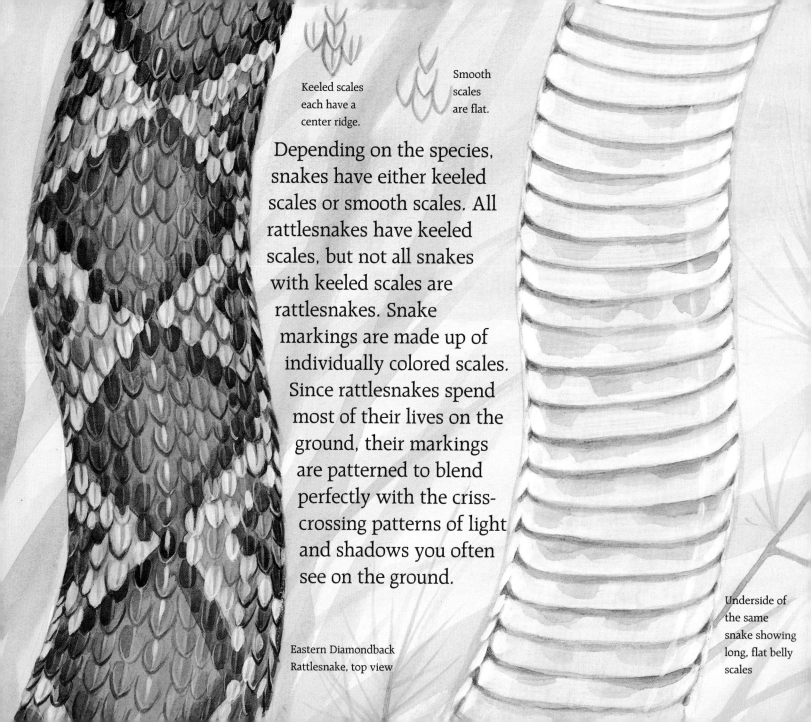

Keeled scales each have a center ridge.

Smooth scales are flat.

Depending on the species, snakes have either keeled scales or smooth scales. All rattlesnakes have keeled scales, but not all snakes with keeled scales are rattlesnakes. Snake markings are made up of individually colored scales. Since rattlesnakes spend most of their lives on the ground, their markings are patterned to blend perfectly with the criss-crossing patterns of light and shadows you often see on the ground.

Eastern Diamondback Rattlesnake, top view

Underside of the same snake showing long, flat belly scales

Close-up look at
flexible belly scales

Snakes move by contracting and expanding powerful muscles under their skin to inch them forward. In addition, the long belly scales are flexible to grasp surfaces and help pull the snake along.

The most distinctive feature of a rattlesnake is its rattle, a series of loosely interlocking hard segments that vibrate whenever the tail shakes. When a rattlesnake rattles, it is warning you not to come any closer or it will bite.

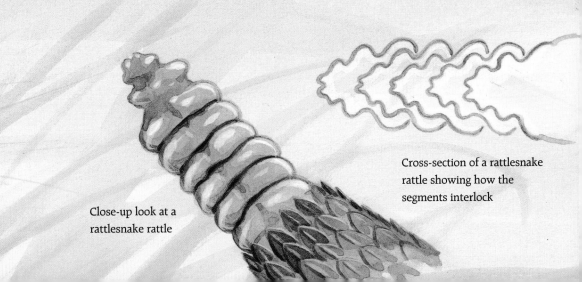

Cross-section of a rattlesnake
rattle showing how the
segments interlock

Close-up look at a
rattlesnake rattle

Snake eyelids are transparent and cover the eyes all the time. A rattlesnake's eye pupils are shaped like tiny footballs. In bright light each pupil narrows to a slit.

A snake's tongue is forked to provide more surface area to collect airborne scent particles. A snake's tongue is not a stinger or a weapon of any kind. It is just a tongue.

Rattlesnakes are members of the pit viper family. Pit vipers have two heat-sensing pits, one on each side of the head, between the eyes and the nostrils. This sixth sense makes it possible for rattlesnakes to locate and catch prey even on the darkest nights.

A rattlesnake's eyesight is very good. Its sense of smell is excellent. Besides being able to smell through nostrils, a snake's tongue picks up particles of dust that the snake senses as a combination of smells and tastes. Rattlesnakes have no ears. They hear with the entire body by feeling sounds vibrating through the ground.

Eastern Diamondback Rattlesnake head (actual size)

Eastern Diamondback Rattlesnake skull (actual size)

When not biting, and when the snake is swallowing prey, rattlesnake fangs fold up to the roof of the snake's mouth. To aid in grasping and holding prey, rattlesnakes also have two long, stationary rows of tiny backward-curving teeth.

Rattlesnakes have two long, hollow teeth called fangs. The fangs work like hypodermic needles to inject a bitten animal with the rattlesnake's poison, called venom. The larger the snake, the more venom it can inject in a single bite. Rattlesnake venom attacks the heart and lung action of its victim. It can be fatal, even to large animals.

Top view of a Timber Rattlesnake head showing bulging cheeks where venom sacs are located inside. The venom sacs are what give the rattlesnake's head its triangular shape.

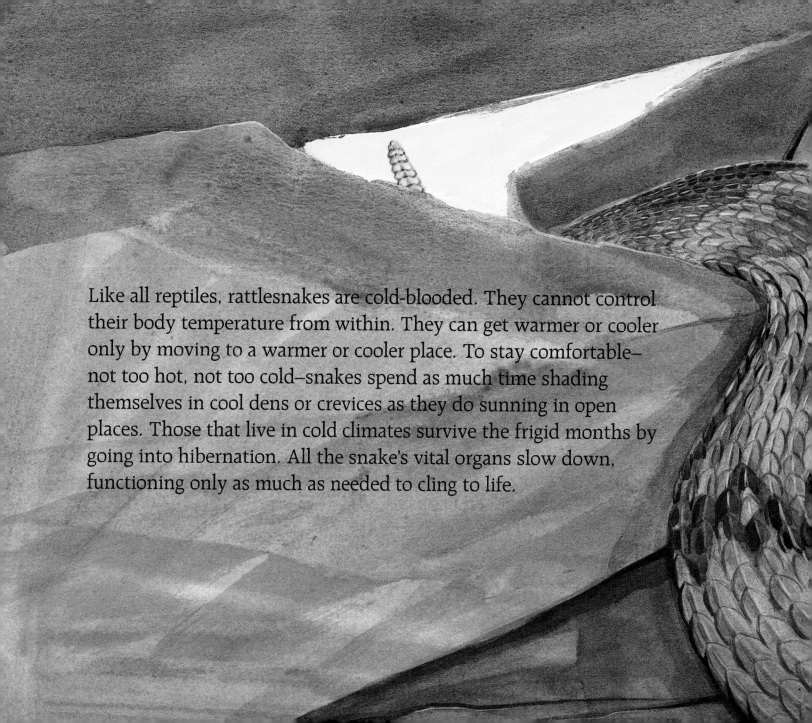

Like all reptiles, rattlesnakes are cold-blooded. They cannot control their body temperature from within. They can get warmer or cooler only by moving to a warmer or cooler place. To stay comfortable– not too hot, not too cold–snakes spend as much time shading themselves in cool dens or crevices as they do sunning in open places. Those that live in cold climates survive the frigid months by going into hibernation. All the snake's vital organs slow down, functioning only as much as needed to cling to life.

Timber Rattlesnake shading itself in a rock den

All rattlesnakes bear live, fully developed young. Depending on the species, rattlesnakes give birth to between three and twenty young rattlesnakes. Rattlesnakes are born in late summer or early fall. Newborns are equipped with fangs and venom.

Dusky Pygmy Rattlesnake and newborns (actual size)

At birth, rattlesnakes have only one rattle segment called a button.

Every snake sheds its skin at least two times a year. Immediately before shedding, a snake's colors become dull, and its markings indistinct. Its eyes are clouded over. After shedding, the same snake is brilliantly colored and strikingly marked. Its eyes are bright and shiny.

A snake sheds its skin to allow for growth and to replace old skin worn thin by all the rubbing and scraping a snake does as it crawls around.

Each time a rattlesnake sheds its skin, it gains an additional segment to its rattle.

A snake crawls out of its skin headfirst.

Shed snakeskin is transparent and colorless.

You cannot tell a rattlesnake's age by counting the number of segments in its rattle because the end segments break off over time.

When threatened, a rattlesnake quickly coils up, head raised, tail rattling. From its coiled position, a rattlesnake can lunge the front third of its body outward and strike with great force. Rattlesnakes also coil to strike their prey.

All snakes swallow their prey whole. Rattlesnakes hunt and eat rodents, small birds, lizards, and frogs.

The rattlesnake's heat-sensing capability can detect and pinpoint prey, even in total darkness, as long as the prey animal's body temperature is warmer than its surroundings.

A rattlesnake's hinged jaws open wide to fit the largest of rattlesnake prey into its mouth.

Small rodents, like this white-footed mouse, are favorite rattlesnake food.

Snakes digest food slowly. After eating, a rattlesnake may not hunt for days. During this time, it becomes sluggish and may barely move. Once a rattlesnake has fully digested a meal, it becomes active again.

Whether resting and digesting or moving along at a top speed of three miles per hour, rattlesnakes blend almost invisibly with their surroundings. They are most often heard rattling before they are seen. And there are times when a rattlesnake strikes first, then rattles!

In rattlesnake areas, watch where you step and watch at least six feet all around you.

Never approach a snake to see if it is a rattlesnake.

Don't run ahead of your family on trails. Never reach up onto ledges or under rocks. Keep your hands out of hollow logs. Be wary of branches or tree trunks lying across a trail–a snake may be on the opposite side. Stay away from roadside ditches. They are favorite hunting places for rattlesnakes. If your family hikes or camps in snake country, carry a snakebite kit and learn how to use it.

Even with their powerful weaponry, rattlesnakes are vulnerable to attack. Roadrunners are birds that regularly eat rattlesnakes. They hop all around a rattlesnake, forcing it to strike repeatedly until it is too tired to strike. Then the roadrunner kills the snake with its strong, sharp beak.

The greatest threat to rattlesnakes comes from us. When we bulldoze and and build in rattlesnake habitat, we drive the snakes out and crowd them onto less and less land. Some people, fearful of rattlesnakes, destroy every one they see. Rattlesnakes are scary and dangerous, but they are also beautiful and highly efficient predators of small animals, especially rodents. Rattlesnakes deserve all the room and respect we can give them—for their well-being, and for ours.

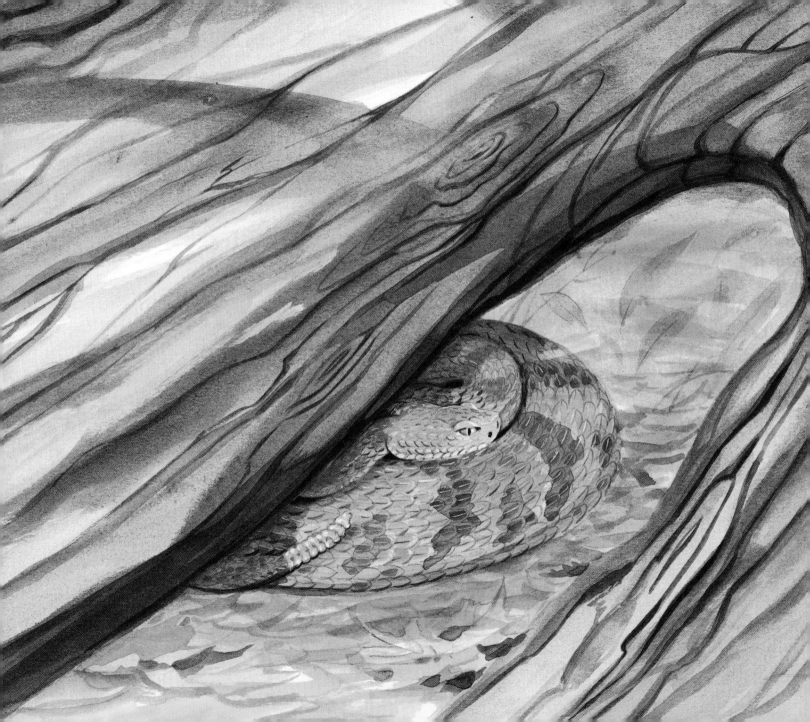

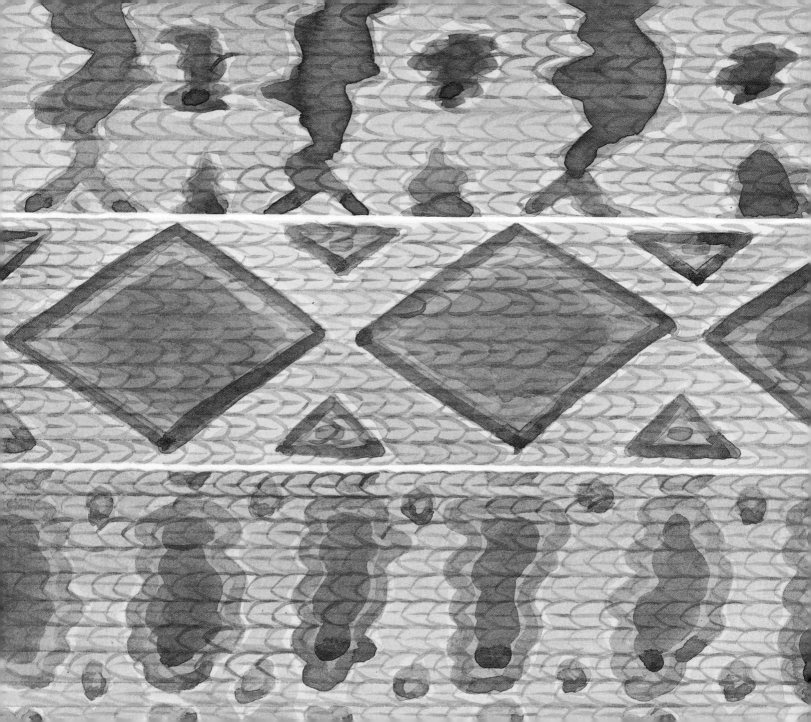

Michelle Sherburne

JIM ARNOSKY is the award-winning author and illustrator of more than 45 books for children. In *All About Rattlesnakes*, he shares his years of observing snakes in the wild. He also traveled to Florida to safely videotape captive rattlesnakes at Homosassa Springs State Wildlife Park.

This is Jim Arnosky's fourth book in his All About series for Scholastic. The first three are *All About Alligators*, *All About Owls*, and *All About Deer*. Each has won awards and two have been named to the American Booksellers Pick of the Lists. Jim Arnosky lives with his family in northern Vermont where there are snakes — not rattlesnakes — living under his porch.